creepy creatures

CONTENTS

Published by Creative Education
P.O. Box 227, Mankato, Minnesota 56002
Creative Education is an imprint of
The Creative Company
www.thecreativecompany.us

Design and production by Ellen Huber
Art direction by Rita Marshall
Printed by Corporate Graphics
in the United States of America

Photographs by 123RF (Alle, Adrian Hillman, Pavel
Konovalov), Art Resource (Cameraphoto Arte, Venice),
Getty Images (Frank Greenaway, Roy Toft), iStockphoto
(Evgeniy Ayupov, Hamiza Bakirci, John Bell, Adam
Gryko, Robert Howell, Eric Isselée, Cathy Keifer, Stefan
Klein, Svetlana Larina, Mihail Orlov, Michael Wesemann),
Shutterstock (Buhantsov Alexey, Fulvio Evangelista,
Robert Adrian Hillman, Eric Isselée, Wendy L. Jarva,
Cathy Keifer)

Library of Congress Cataloging-in-Publication Data
Bodden, Valerie.
Spiders / by Valerie Bodden.
p. cm. — (Creepy creatures)
Summary: A basic introduction to spiders, examining
where they live, how they grow, what they eat, and
the unique traits that help to define them, such as
their ability to spin silk threads and webs.
Includes index.
ISBN 978-1-58341-996-0
1. Spiders—Juvenile literature. I. Title. II. Series.
QL458.4.B66 2010
595.4'4—dc22   2009052522
CPSIA: 040110 PO1135

First Edition
9 8 7 6 5 4 3 2 1

spiders

VALERIE BODDEN

CREATIVE EDUCATION

You walk into your yard on a sunny morning. Drops of water cover the grass. You notice a spider web sparkling in the sunlight. Nearby is a spider!

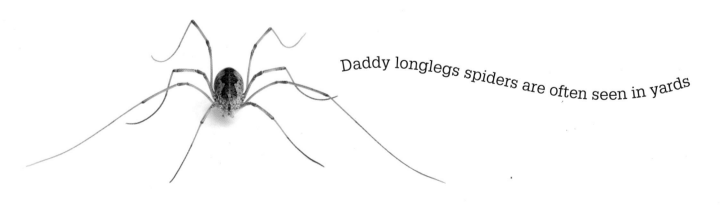

Daddy longlegs spiders are often seen in yards

Spiders are **arachnids** (*uh-RAK-nids*). Their bodies have two main parts. Spiders have eight legs. Most spiders have eight eyes, too. At the back of their bodies, spiders have two to six **organs** called spinnerets. The spinnerets make a kind of thread called silk.

Some spiders are smaller than the tip of a pencil. Others are as big as a plate! Many spiders are brown or black. But some are red, yellow, or green.

Some spiders are spotted or more than one color

Garden spiders (right) are much smaller than tarantulas (above)

There are more than 35,000 different kinds of spiders. Black and yellow garden spiders can be found in many places. Tarantulas (*tuh-RAN-choo-luhz*) are big, hairy spiders.

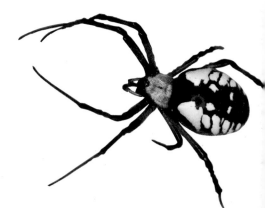

Spiders live almost everywhere! They make their homes in forests, deserts, and grasslands. Spiders have to watch out for **predators**. Birds, lizards, and centipedes all eat spiders.

Frogs may eat small spiders

Some mother spiders lay one egg. Others lay more than 1,000 eggs! Baby spiders look like small adult spiders. As they grow, they get too big for their skin. They **molt** so they can keep growing. Many spiders live for about a year. But some tarantulas can live more than 20 years.

After spiders hatch from their eggs (left), sometimes they ride on their mother's back (above)

Spiders eat **insects**. Some big spiders also eat frogs! Many spiders catch their food in a web. Others chase their prey, or the animals they eat. Spiders bite their prey with sharp, **poisonous** teeth called fangs.

A spider called the green lynx eats bees

Spider silk is very strong. Spiders use it to make webs. They also wrap it around their eggs to keep them safe. Baby spiders even use silk "balloons" to float to new homes.

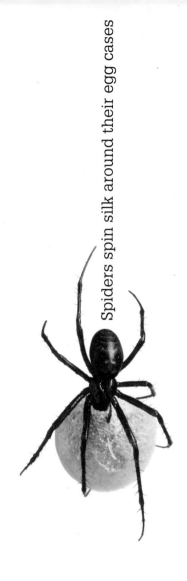

Spiders spin silk around their egg cases

Long ago, people in Greece said that a girl was turned into a spider that could weave beautiful webs. People in Africa told stories about tricky spiders. It can be fun finding and watching these eight-legged creepy creatures!

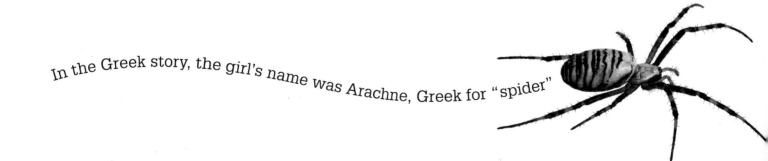

In the Greek story, the girl's name was Arachne, Greek for "spider"

MAKE A SPIDER WEB

You can make your own spider in a web! First cut
8 pieces of yarn, each about 10 inches (25 cm) long.
Glue the yarn to a piece of paper in a web pattern.
Then use finger paint to make a thumbprint on the
paper. This is your spider's body. Make a pinky print
next to it. This is the head.
When the paint is dry, use
a marker to draw eight
legs on the body.

GLOSSARY

arachnids: small, eight-legged animals like spiders and scorpions

insects: small animals with three body parts and six legs; most have two pairs of wings, too

molt: to lose a shell or layer of skin and grow a new, larger one

organs: body parts that do certain jobs; for example, eyes are organs for seeing

poisonous: filled with something that can hurt or kill other animals or people if it gets into their body

predators: animals that kill and eat other animals

READ MORE

Franks, Katie. *Spiders Up Close*. New York: PowerKids Press, 2008.

Hartley, Karen, Chris Macro, and Philip Taylor. *Spiders*. Chicago: Heinemann Library, 2008.

WEB SITES

Enchanted Learning: Spiders
http://www.enchantedlearning.com/subjects/arachnids/spider/Spiderprintout.shtml
Learn more about spiders and print a spider picture to color.

The Field Museum Underground Adventure: Meet the Creepy Critters
http://www.fieldmuseum.org/underground adventure/critters/critter_info.shtml
Read fun facts about wolf spiders.